BEING ON THE MOON

BEING ON THE MOON

MOON

Annharte

POLESTAR
BOOK PUBLISHERS

BEING ON THE MOON

Copyright © 1990 by Marie Annharte Baker
All rights reserved

Published by
Polestar Press Ltd., R.R. 1, Winlaw, B.C., V0G 2J0, 604-226-7670

Distributed by
Raincoast Book Distribution Ltd., 112 East 3rd Avenue,
Vancouver, B.C., V5T 1C8, 604-873-6581

Canadian Cataloguing in Publication Data
Baker, Marie Annharte, 1942-
Being on the moon
Poems.
ISBN 0-919591-52-3
I. Title.
PS8553.A44B4 1990   C811'.54   C90-091152-2
PR9199.3.B34B4 1990

Acknowledgements
Published with the assistance of the Canada Council
and the Saskatchewan Arts Board

A portion of this collection has previously appeared in *Backbone,
Conditions, Fireweed, Prairie Fire,* and *Seventh Generation,*
and been heard on *Ambience.*

Edited by Allan Safarik
Cover author photograph by La Vision Photography, Regina
Photo tinting by Jim Brennan
Produced by Polestar Press in Winlaw, B.C.
Printed and bound in Canada

MEGWETCH

To be an old bag you need: my mom and her generation who did not see 36 plus; sass from Little Saskatchewan relations; Allan Safarik and other writer buddies who don't just see me as "the Indian"; strong Anishinabe women who are my sisters and mothers; white women who have worn out their welcome on me or are just wearing; white sisters who have endured my ferocity, pms fits & my latest addictions; my son Forrest Funmaker who makes it fun to be a mom; my father, Lawrence Baker, who took over being a mom; and anyone who has admired our moon calendar, Enheduanna for instance, and wondered what it's like Being On The Moon.

Nokomis Blessing Us All.

CONTENTS

LACEY MOON

The immigrants brought all their finery
They put it on their couch arms or back
Their doilies were either limp or starched
Tiny holes made of thread covered up velvety
Undersides exposed but the end tables had lamps
The coffee tables had to guard against
Beer bottle rings or ashtrays of butts
Which spilled as clodhopper feet were rested

It's strange to wear a doily on your face
It doesn't look charming like a veil
Your face turned to the side appears shy
Something's cooking when you do that
I'm not about to trust your monias ways
Not much snow this winter on the ground
The dark patchwork latticed white spots
Cover up goings on even yellow piss
Won't last long until spring laundry time

SMUDGE

Fume of sweetgrass strikes
coiling in my brain
connecting me between ears

Burning braid stays lit
carried in an abalone shell
making us all tidy & neat

Preening in public so dowdy
poke a little under my arm
a plug of incense for keeps

Dusted off my man jealousy
better keep my eye glued
that bitch gets too smart

Dowse that eye for now
spectacles keep my nose in line
someone hid a dried beaver ball

My mouth needs an overhaul
give my puckered up lips
Saturday night sweet as jam

Tilt my smile so my face
doesn't get stretch marks
let out all my pretend laughs

Those dusty webs in my heart
have a clever design in the weave
let the spider mind her net

Pull out all my fears
how baby teeth got yanked
with a black loop of thread

Where were we, you & me
once on the braided rug
rattling my cage for a cure

STAY OUT OF THE WOODS

These woods I know are mine
rock faces stare out at me
blasted out for the train
cursed they swear original
colours given green with rust
ochre streaks moss patches
frozen lake with coarse veins
eagle flying over the train
might clench feet for warmth
or choose not to wear out
her grip on two months pests
summer takes over Ontario

Guess to whom the woods belong
rock faces scream leave us alone
the city people don't know much
bush is outside lakes of shapes
skinny jack pine holding a rock
his cone blown far from memory
he shades his rock temple base
the silence of the angular mouths
picking on you in this church
graffiti's hit them smack dab
the way priest sermons marked
words to grow up dwelling on

PENUMBRA

for Betty

Temporary the shade my straw hat weaves
across my basket face of Caribe pleasure.
The bright sun makes me want to run and jump,
I had been told if I were smart, I'd stay hidden.
On my island, I keep to myself & lie around.
Turtles crawl past me to dig their nests.
Tortuga oil is outlawed and so am I.

Odd, this exposure of my not too recent killing.
Seventeen years it took getting to court
those who mashed my face because of dark skin.
Hating the contrast of each pinky penis
I left The Pas to be a turista and relax

They understand I stayed away to make sure
I'm not the only witness to their sorry act.
Not even good at it, I might add as insult.
The reserve is a huge donut around the town,
no place to go unless you're Indian like me.
Laughing at the other end of the beach
gets me wondering how it's my turn.

NO SHAME

Indian pride spoken here
Fried baloney served for lunch
Chinese food to go

○

SKINNY MOON

My skinny bowl like you with thin skin
A shell without a turtle; necklace bust
A snake rattle left or grey neglected bone
Dried out sponge ends with flaky dust
My kettle long ago was greased-up fine
Enough for all to dig in seconds for weeks
Take home leftovers in your handy pail
Bannocks, frybreads, round out our menu
Doing without feeding I fast without visions
Going on without you I just hunger the feels
Absent minded I crave   I give in   smoke up
Grabbing a hand, a kid, a lover, a beer
The only place to go is downtown to climb up
A kiddy slide in city park slip down forgot how
Slick on your skeleton of rubbery gristle
(I liked to chew on) tipping-up for thrills
My back tendency is sliding out baring nerves
Other ways hang on fast for dear life greedy
Keeping me from flipping over sideways on a beach
Bleaching my whalebone for commercial sake

GRANNY GOING

Granny going on the road to town
Packing her raggy clothes on her back
Tied up in a plastic garbage bag
Walking the one road through the bush
To her gang on the streets calling
Charming her bone crack marrow
An old dog tagged behind her every step
Too scared to be scaring a bear
He would know she needed company
He heard her wine gut grinding

END OF THE TRAIL

Blue Thunder got in a brag
    How he filled his water bottle
    To mix his Lysol
Scotty was a door man
    He passed out by hospital doors
    Let people step over him
    Going to an A.A. meeting
    Each bump on his face schemed
Uninvited, the River People
    Came to feast, on food not blessed
    Two hot dogs hung in one mouth
    Paper plates were heaped up
Giving tobacco to a Grandma
    She begged for cigarettes
    Staggering on the street
    My daughter is a teacher, she said
    I'm okay, I need a place to stay

GOOD MOANING

How I moan so but I am
not moaning so much as
I used to moan in times past
I moaned and groaned not
so much at having sex
but the other marital
acts I performed
but now my moan is low
so much to say slow
more of the same moan
this be a boring moan
I am not done in by it

My moaning friend called
just this morning to say
she was dead — drunk
as she was but she began
her awful moan at life
I groaned in chorus the way
a throat singer pitches
after moaning and groaning
I took off on a jigging tune
she stayed on groaning

SQUEEZE POEM

His weapon a dick to kill the insides of women
alone I ache jitters if the phone rings I'll
be grateful how easy to meander into cowpie
on path nuance writes about the weather blow
by blow routine phone rang once I thought an
intruder little curiosity who called reporting
on my self is not a good idea 100 porcupine
needles pain my nose convincing hermit I chased
my tail today barking about it compassion milks
me such a squeeze peach seducing me night chant
becomes a song of an army of women giving birth
in a jar poetry pours out of my pores I talked
to a lion in my dream who was my pet who told
me to set him free in the wild he would become
impounded by the city even as exotic he is I was
to give him a ride to the outskirts of town or
give him a 1 way to Africa I was nude he hungry

MOON BEAR

My moon is a deep lake in mind
little fishes swim in depths
too scared to see the shaking
sunlight spears above their stare
She-bears birthing in my winter womb
sleeping till spring to growl again
shadows dancing before the nights come
Tomorrow the wind message will bring
what happened since her earth eyes shut
Muzzle up and around for scents secure
Maybe even a tourist campout is early
Her baby wants her back, it's still cold
The iceface feel of my moon lake
slips away as soon as there is more sun
My moon will grow within me to greet
rising bears bringing warm faces to my lips

PINCHED AWAKE

Pinched for time up against the wall
blood red lips break apart
drop your eyes to the crushed velvet
Navajo blouse with silver conchos
She needs a leech to drink the swelling
from her face
lips caved in   mashed strawberry jello
Her nose is not bruised so I get some sleep
I want to find a cloth for her lips
Tomorrow if I stop running away
she'll start talking
I'm sure awake

MY MOTHER WAS DARK

I didn't seem to notice. I had to ask
one day about Indians. Maybe I heard
that word. God, she said, baked people.
The whiteman was half-baked. Indians
were the right color not burnt or overdone. I knew her color was perfect.

MOTHER RITE

She had to go out and do a man's job;
leaving me with a teapot to embroider. It's
blue thread on a white sack. Our teapot just
sat on the stove brewing titanic acid. She
must've been bored looking after me so she
wanted to work with my dad. I finished my
first sewing lesson proudly. She cut her
foot with the axe that day.

'50's HANGOUT

She was comfy in the '50s-style Chinese
restaurant remembering all the cafes on
Main Street in Winnipeg. She even knew
the Moon Cafe, my favorite name.

She dug her fork into Banana Cream Pie
as I thought about her sugar problem.
Never mind, she indulged. Her fork
was held with her index finger extended.
It had been broken and never mended.
She could give a finger without knowing it.
Her face had the scars but with wrinkles
nature became kind to her expression.

She talked about some of the women that
had gone to the same boarding school.
One had become a corporate lawyer still
a big drunk though. Her face was shot.
Being a beauty, age made her more equal.
Another was a nurse, but again a doper.
These sophisticates, we sighed, chewing.

She was size 42 in her blouses. She wanted
to cover her stomach. Her jumbo size seemed
more because of her massive shoulders. She
must have been a terror drinking. The perm
hid her thinning and partly greying hairdo.
Now 60, she was still attractive as an elder.

Her old drinking chum was near death. He
wanted to spend his last days at her side.
The booze wasn't killing him, it was cigarettes.
They made spots on his lungs, the doctors

said could be fixed. She always wondered why all her old men were sick or dying. I teased her, at least she had three to worry about.

She saw white people in their more perverted ways. While drinking, she had witnessed the parade of politicians around a gay hang-out in Winnipeg called the Legislative Buildings. Maybe the "golden boy" was their good luck charm. She saw all the regulars who picked up their lovers. Once shoes were left on the river bank. She and her old man almost took them but they might have become too involved in the investigation once the body was found in the river. Only two gay guys from her reserve were known publicly.

CHASING MOON

Safely sitting in a dark space, an idol so
Pleased with herself and that granny grin
Teasing me and making me howl her down tonight
While I have rest before running to light a fire
When I'm not looking a baby moon swells my sides
Surprise to me my belly puffs up so jeans get small
Breeding again as the bothering moon circles above
Waiting through the pain that my brain doesn't fit
Choosing calamity is knowing the moon will crash
Cradles of her children crushed in a collision
I forget the scare of my granny's visit
I stop the burning of my heart and let her feel
The baby bump and promise me to chase my clan

SQUAW BEAT

There's going to be an Indian war
They won't call me a squaw no more
Beside the riverbanks drumming waves
Brown bags wrap up my dreams pouring
But who will listen to this sob story?
Squaws on Main Street won't keep silent
Chanting the ghost song in my ears
Out tickling fears, out screaming scars
Tuning out all tears, keeps me sipping beer

NIGHT CHANT

Shouts penetrate feathers in my pillow
passing through from the wall bouncing
flip back right into a ceremonial jar
Piercing walls now early morning comes sad
returning at night strange squeals shock me
giggling voices from the jar after a wake
drum beats pick-up, suits me fine, even my groan
Seasons begin with song, must now be spring
my Noxema jar sure came in handy, a sardine tin
would do for a visitation as dreaming goes
Different news views reviews were in telling
ancient aunties chitchat chanting a baby name

MY CRICKET GOT AWAY

A young intelligent man conversing about ridding
his house of crickets smoothed the touchdown
at Regina airport
He had snuffed his in a jar with Raid
I confessed I took my one invader cricket
in a margarine tub to a parking lot
First I had sympathy
I caught him changing his coat at my place
I mistook him for a cockroach having sex
until I began to notice his partner wasn't moving at all
Will grasshoppers take over the city or will Indians
(Moving as often as they do, having sex frequently)
take over the whole province from the farmers
when they pay us back for dumping pesticides?
Once landed my questions are still in the air
if there is one big cricket on the horizon   I pity him

GETTING EVEN ON CUSTER

She tags around his public appearances
sitting up front her legs wide open /
right out of his book / a fat squaw

    She was a goalie waiting /
    hockey doesn't bring out
    the best in a man / cab driving's
    letting the meter run up

    would we be better off
    if he took his fare?

    he's telling us stories / White Dog
    Party Chief Bumming Around

    never heard about it
    conceited Indians
    gave up victory
    easily
    for rides

    Thunder-Dancer / out-of-step
    outside his cab
    taught him
    a good revenge
    writing Indian stories

    Picture / Yellow Hair
    Yellow Hair
    in her teeth
    waking up

    she ripped a damn good
    cowboy shirt / blue satin
    fringed like a shawl
    she made ribbons

for her trophy shawl
the leather pants
were too hot in bed

She needed to use his leather
for her crafts

Frankensquaw / coming soon
to your neighborhood theatre

HOOKER MOON

Big wads grab her greedy eyes
Small change no tricks worth playing
Cops bother her only she's looking
For her sister living in the north end
Funny address she lost at the last hotel
Couple of twenties stuck in her bra
Cashy night here comes another boozer
She sings Roll with me Henry tonight
Share a lodge for a suitcase of beer
Just wiggle into a moss-lined cradle
Handicrafted with quill; lullaby extra
Cosy up mister around her fire
See footprints of her brothers' war dancing

A WOMAN'S FISH-HOOK STORY

A big jackfish arrives, all cleaned up.
Ready for frying. Everyone drops by.
Even the new Chief. I'm back visiting.
At my cousin's place, her daughter helps.
Not me because I'm her yearly visitor.
I just sit around and talk with them.
A woman's baby was born with a copper wire
on his head. We make interrogative O's.
Then my niece says she lost her IUD.
Even the doctor couldn't find it. Mystery.
I tease her by saying that there's one guy
in Little Sandy Bay who must be wearing it.

HUDSON BAY BILL

after so many years
Rupert wants me to pay
a bill   but he owes me

I am still for the most part
savage   my credit is no good
my fur is gone before I get it
I'm just a skin so bare

my story exploring history
is not told   I was not
in the way until somewhat old

trappers liked my dark face
settlers did make a good party
their wives properly hid

dangerous touching trinkets
jumped   put in a jail claim
I stole those in my underwear

my way of being honest
is doubtful as heaven
I want a fair share not
what I end up begging

EXCHANGE CAFE

Growing up in a Chinese restaurant is ethnic
When first the word was out it might shut down
I had to ask where will Main Street Indians go?
I still see cleavers chasing, hear strange cursing
My mouth knows what is the Soup of the Day
One time this guy said Poon Tang to us girls
We ran home scared because we didn't know Chinese

DARKLOVE

at night...you get dark feelings...for a dark lover...at day-
time it goes...darkloving...gives anyone...a cherry...abc
teachers...do it at my office...do it in school...streets are
free...boozecans charge so much...crazy talk seductions...
need figuring out...eyes wink wild...them bellies lean on
me...tonight will come so slow...save it my love...stretch
my reach...chalk up this...charming my words...no
fumbles at sex...boarding school boyfriend look alike...
sames jokes crack...look down on me...white lying...so
I'm chiefless...remind me

JUMPER MOON

My turquoise junker taking the path
Through the plains of short grass descended
From the six foot high blades that buffalo
Brushed aside as they picked out Indians

There were some stalking but those woolly heads
Knew they were hiding, it was just a little game
These two silly deer raced my car   I saw tails
Sailing by, thanking them for being good runners

Hooves on my windshield would have paled me
Too many bloody fur spots on the road
Summer and nighttime slows them down to a crawl
Rocks would jump if blinded, if bothered

Mothers hide daughters from even a nosy neighbor
As big and little sisters they protect each other
Huddling before the flashing light of a police beam
Soothing down the terror of investigation

What if they find something wrong, they always do
Saving a little body is to turn on it, saying
I'm no good and neither are you to them who ask
Show you what it's about   jumping over the moon

GYPSY FIX

In this no man's land a gypsy fortune teller
promises that for three thousand dollars cash
I will receive total psychic joy.
A bit pricey this alteration of my darker self,
instead I get my truck fixed. Done, feminized.
A farmer had fiddled with her motor one spring
coupling her with an absolutely wrong alternator.
Warned repeatedly it might drop out unexpectedly
as I drove dusty roads I accepted the severity
of her manifold problem and enjoyed greasy men
hanging over her hood talking about her Y pipe
curved and connected under her body nodding to me
their approval while I practised the proper names
a junk dealer needs to find the exact part to fit.

THAT CACTUS BITCH

She liked the move to this tree-scarce
country. Stood only an inch high in her
green plastic pot. I admired her calm
bravery as she sat up in the front seat
of my Pinto station wagon.

After two years of hot radiator steam
hissing and my failure to adjust the valve
properly, she gave no complaint whatsoever.
In fact, it was to her liking.

She's sporting two buds on her sides while
giving me a grateful and gratifying silhouette
Grown twice as big since we moved out west.
That heat wave wilted me.

She's been a loyal and trusting companion
throughout all our drought years together.
Never had any reason to be wary of her with
me except for one spring I got careless.

She had more spines than I imagine on a
cat dick. Maybe I handled her a bit too rough.

SIX SISTERS

Where do they come from, all directions?
I get out of bed to see a red son rising.
Spirit sisters beg of me to be a daredevil.
I'm not. Just another crybaby. I defy
All my mother's keepers who advise me
Take in one more. Charge the Earth!
We get the dirt treatment. Defiled. Down.
Damn do-gooder in me keeps me rolling over
Nights I don't sleep well. Last night!
Rolled without my money gone. Megwetch.
Spared. Not changed. I suppose healing
(pawning the pipe of our daughters' dreaming)
Is another pose. Silver hair is worthless.
If you want, you may take my turquoise ring.
I'm sick of showing it off to you sisters.

BIRD CLAN MOTHER

Middle of my junk room
    Dream eyes seeing small
        Prehistoric possum mother

Running footbeats jiggling
    Babies hanging on a long tail
        Curved over her back

What was chasing
    My little friend
        Just before dinner?

She could be running
    Right into some bad
        Stink mouth to be gulped

Down with Family Style Gravy
    To be a bird dropping
        Better to choose a cannibal cure

Another time dream eyes clear
    White bird place known to be
        For all birds a home

Beating wings roaring
    Coming closer starting to lift
        Rising and soaring high above

Lying at peace on a bird back
    How did I get here so fast?
        My wings hardly moved at all

Soft feathers fanning me
    The scars from the possum past
        Still hot from toothmarks

Gliding like a Bird Clan Mother
   I did take off wherever to begin
      Crafty ways, I hunt myself

Whoever sees my shadow overhead
   Knows to run but I slow up
      Beady little eyes blink quick

Ducking the flying jokes I resume
   The feeble crouch run and hide
      This once I will eat squash blossoms

MAYAN MOON

Running down up escalator
Turnabout zip down tag
Shopper trance is broken briefly
Who needs to watch kids scrambling?
Pissed off when foot is scrunched
Moccasins keep coming undone
Slight injury slows up my parade
Minding my old lady steps

The flat top looks ever flashy
Hazy ring edging around the moon
Making her princess entrance
About time she showed — Indian time
Sparkling glass tiara on tilt
Used tires on lawns turned inside
Out may grow wild flower gardens
Silver paint job hides a used look
Cut spiky like the tiara on her hair

My looks offend righteous instincts
It's so handy to carry sunglasses
Pushed from behind into a left stance
Keep your place in rankfile girly
The movement moves ahead together big mama
These high tops were given to me
They seem so baggy my foot comes out
My aunt made them for a bigfoot not me
Not what I should wear for grand entry

Senorita, amiga gorda your siesta
She is waiting by the temple, what next?
Funny no pension no tours given
All you hear is a PA system turned on

Easy to impress me even about jumping off
Once I make it to the top meditating
The many triggers of thinking alone
Who was there with me to confide myself?

Only at your turn leap to the right
Over the well at Mayapa first deep go
Without a push dive muskrat dive
Below a turtle napping be sure to bring
More mud on your way back up keemootch
Say would you buy that order?
Ever a sneaky hint of how it gets done
Virgins drown a wicked thirst
Before they ride with jaguars
The Amazon is full of them

PRETTY TOUGH SKIN WOMAN

old dried out meat piece
preserved without a museum
missing a few big rips
her skin was guaranteed

her bloomers turned grey
outliving the city washing
not enough drinks to keep her
from getting home to the bush

tough she pushed bear fat down
squeezed into sally ann clothes
she covered up her horny places
they tried sticking her under

soft jelly spots remain in bone
holding up this pretty tough hide
useful as a decorated shield for baby
swinging in her sweet little stink

just smell her old memories, gutted fish
baked muskrat — she saw a lady
in a shopping mall with a fur coat
told her an Indian must eat such delicacies

her taste was good she just needed a gun
to find a room in the city to put down
her beat-up mattress where her insides fell out
visitors ate up the bannock drank her tea

they were good at hocking her radio or tv
everywhere she stopped she told her troubles
if I press my ear down on this trail I bet
I'll be able to hear her laughing and gabbing

TRAPPER MOTHER

Looking into the animal den, I saw how carefully she
set the trap hidden with pieces of pine branches. Our
tracks she kicked away in the snow. I was her helper.
She gave me the job of turning the wheel on the egg
beater to make milk from Klim powder. The meals I made
were for the cat. She supervised boiling birds in
my toy cookware after I'd plucked them. I wasn't very
squeamish. I saw my mother's bloodied hands on a muskrat
skin turning it inside out to fit a stretcher. Her floured
hands made a baby pig from the scraps of bannock dough.
Her tomato soup was creamy because she used canned milk.
The only time I tasted it was after school. I came home
knowing she was acting strange. She just wasn't around
that much or she was drunk a lot. In the bush, we had a
stove and table next to the bed. In the city, the
room had a double burner hot plate. I never saw my mother
in a kitchen but I saw her in jail.

EVERYTHING ELSE IS ON HOLD

a social worker may sit listening straining to hear foreign
speech as when you speak Canadian you do not draw
attention except when very drunk you say f-f-f but English
talkers brag they hear "hoose yr worker" not whose
worker are you spoken

When the ice starts out chippy hockey sticks will nick you
I'm tapped by her eyes double ringers yellow under violet
bruisings as she asks "Did you see a little boy standing
here?" "I must be seeing a ghost" I hear she had a story
I want to tell

have to follow her ask her who she was and he was
if she knew I am a ghost writer knowing about the lives
in the recent past a shriek & holler to my being undone
forgot what natural dignity keeps you from down & outers
not ghosts just knew me back when

the Aztec princess drops in my Mayan mood evolves
demanding her sacrifice my throat cut so poems will gasp
out above throttle humming may drive her away I know
she likes rock music best she dances acid stoned at my
son's air guitar playing licks

that bitch will find out what I want she haunts bumming
a ride on my hump back surgery or herbal tea won't affect
piggy back no genuine sow will treat me like I'm her grand
cadillac tires puffed up her homemade sandals won't get
a worn look

I visit my friend's mother who just quit drinking to ask her
about the ghost in her daughter's dream; is it her brother
we drink tea to us she may not see my ghost or cannibal
just a mosquito woman drinking me up I hate to ask too
much today

DOWN SOUTH

Who said work was for us
my job is being an Indian squaw
they ask me to put in my time
a game they call me Minnie Ha Ha
there are no more jobs down south
rich women want to keep our kids
for a hobby   scrubbing extra hard
to make them white until their teens
bring out that ol' Southern Comfort
Canada lady   so again a squaw will laugh
I like my job in Indian country
no white woman tell me what I do

ROOTING MOON

Promise me biting wike is believing
The seneca digs were worth bug stings
Coming into town with a bunch in my hand
Seneca snaker roots sold for a quarter
Brown bag of store candy bought ginseng
    my dad's word it was
    aspirin for white people
    he was white so okay
You had to boil it up not chew on it
Wagons were for riding but horses weren't
Medicine children working didn't fix it
Summers were for seneca root digging
    getting sick on bad water
    accidently cured myself
    drank Pepsis all day
Nobody said you have medicines children
Just kept us digging it out of the dirt
The roots got washed & sun dried slow
Put in a few gunny sacks stacked up

TRYING HARDER

In the movies I spent my childhood for 15 cents
on a dream for a day. Most will admit
they cheered for the troops to wipe out
Indians. I wanted Geronimo to win
Cochise to kick ass & they did it for me
yelling all by myself at the show but
I screamed when I saw the Indian dancing fast
forward which the old movies speeded up
to look like jumping. Trying to be
Indian at day camp was disgusting, our leader
told us kids to make tipis, play Indian.
I made an African hut, a long house
weaved of twigs & leaves, a basket house
to be proud of my Native left over land.
Geronimo, Cochise taught me to fight

EN VISCERA

for Bea Medicine

Chicken dogs bark loud
chasing phantom intruders
old-timers kept dog company
watching the mammoth herds
tusking trees nudging noses
shedding shag ears flapping
a rez-dog life is mean
dog soup is served in a feast
mean dogs must get singed
deer or rabbits are boiled
spoons bust flour lumps open
inside each one, a powder puff
my first plate of tripe
quivering honeycombs steaming
shook up my insides proper

COME TO MY SHACK

what makes a shack a shack?
a rabbit makes a shack a shack
where do rabbits come from?
the snares my mother set   in her kindness
didn't use the label hares or snowshoes
the elegant Peter Rabbit whom I met in school
didn't come to our shack
his cousin Jack Waboose visited us
my snowshoes were my feet running on hard snow
the landscape temporary by noon I would sink
I did meet the Great Wabasso in school selling sheets
he sat on his great white road
leaving no raisin trails behind
he was easy to draw   no clothes   no watches
he sat in my pictures naked
log houses wrap around you
tipi poles stacked   chinked with moss
blue tin stove cooked my side three times
I was learning about leaning on the stove
which cooked rabbits that came to our shack

POWWOW LIGHT COMPANY

Tip toe heel toe
Each foot coming down
Winding in a big circle of trails
Promenade right all the time
No handgrabbing in a square
Behind us a head dancer dangling tails
Some jump in and shake the floor
They forgot how to walk and wiggle
Ancestors hear the drum
Each foot has its own power
Steam irons with holes shooting air
Holding even the fatty jingle dress dancer
Indian technology works fine
Moccasin Power, Dancing Power
We light up the sky, each others face
Jump in Indians, don't be shy

PEACHY MOON

Fuzz stuck to my face, figure to proceed
with caution past the guard hairs, digging
all my feet into the undergrowth for balance
Same scenario, me on the job, lonesome boss
crawling like a tick   dragging my raisin body
sinking my tube tongue
piercing easily the ripe redness
without much added pressure my harvesting
this dented, still usable peach, continues.
Summer camps now empty   rutted roads still
tempt shoppers   visit a pub
tie down kinships remember names
relocated renewed redone relations   nomadism leaves
before fall after we finish up tea made
on this trip sweetie let's jump out dump
the car run in the ditch fly the coop
You end up taking up all the room we're so
pinched for space Harvester of all I missed
pulling back as I move up to you floating
out in front I missed even the bruisings
touché my Teacher no offence but you got
swollen up skin so what keeps your mushy red
striped stone inside   my buddies are all kind
they give away packed tight in a jar
peaches snuggling close up peach pictures
on cans were my choice put up pasted along
with bartlett pears   ladies in a parlor
drinking tea creamed peaches were prettier
if shaved   Changing Woman sees a fallen peach
by a tree she asks because she knows who
owns this cute vagina it's not the first
time she was present at her births
she doesn't get too serious she laughs herself
stuck full of hair eyelashes nail-tearings

RUB UP ME RECIPE

Rub up me some more
Rub me up right now
Rub up me so good
Rub me up with song
Rub up me a recipe
We sing to get along
Press me flat bannock down
Poking little holes all around
Take out the lard when I'm done
Grab that spoon & have some fun

I GET DIRTY

this crab's for you
half a crayfish left
chokecherries I'll smash
for you with women stones

my cowrie lips gnaw inside
your very berry nub

use my moho
n. borehole into
the Earth's crust
as far as the m.

apply my product
to your palm
rub hands together
work through with fingers

this rich cream works
like an invisible glove

apply with upward
and downward strokes
over face and throat
repeat this
until no trace
of makeup or dirt

RUMMAGE MAN

You have been used
Like this old pair of shorts
With the elastic gone
Holding you up to the light
I see holes in you
Those spots about to go
You want to wear me out
I want to patch you up
A heart, a star, a diamond
Sure spade design on you
So when you sit down
You won't get cold
Old, hard, carried away
You are my antique find
X-wino, X-con, X-cop,
X-teacher, X-preacher
When you get to be my turn
You are always an X-man
It's my habit to shop around
Let me look this over once

BOOB STRETCH

my breasts when I was 14 were silky soft
to the touch from outside my brassiere
loaded with scarves to avoid the falsie feel
babies know what to do right away just suck
choosing between vanilla on the right doodoos
or chocolate on the left doodoos
just have to be plugged in
someday we will all have the granny tits
eaten out milkers stretched by generations
so long and flat over our shoulders trailing

SCRIBBLE MOON

Shiny circle of spit stuck between lines
Picky words dictated in a hypnotic state
Each mouthful must imitate pictographs
Near a waterfall, spray painted by her lips

Power spot recognition brings her homing
Moving on to the next great spark of fireball
Hey boy, a grandfather made a joke on her
Messing with the striker of her typing machine

She sticks in, hitting all the keys hard
Each thought will be safe as spider rope
She stashes the scraps under a coffee table
Wonders why the whitener gets so thick

Many cross-out arrows in her scribbler record
Disturbed sleep patterns of who stays up
Puttering around looking outside she notices
The moon's scarred face has vanished

UPBRAID

Some New York whiteguy cops a free admission to an
Indian museum on account of he's married to an Indian
wife. I look on their map worried that my tribe is not
official & find the Saulteaux stretch well marked even to
the tundra. I thought we hung around cities. I sign in even
though Bungi is also a recognized tribe. There is a special
Bungi card which I've picked out to send to a friend who
knows there's no such thing. "We can always be Bungis if
our reserves won't have us," is my cheery note for the lost
years. She will laugh just as if I said, "rabbit choker."
I would need patience before saying, "dogeater" to anyone
but in time I would. Wannabees take a lot of time to joke.
We buffalo all their attempts to be our nichimooses.
Maybe in my last years I will even defy this black neighborhood which houses our heritage. I'll put on my beaded
barrette, grasping the grey hairs, hike into the big city with
my flappy house dress. I will be taken for an old white
lady on a vacation, having proven my blood by climbing
to Machu Picchu for the view.

RACED OUT TO WRITE THIS UP

I often race to write   I write about race   why do I write
about race   I must erase all trace of my race   I am an
eraser abrasive bracing myself embracing

it is classic to want to write about class   not low class but
up the nose class   I know I am classy   brassy   crass ass
of a clash comes when I move up a rung

we are different skins   different bins for brown rice and
white rice   not even a container of wild rice   you know
what they do when you are white and not rich   poverty
counts big when you count the cost of a caste a colorful
past

drunk as a skunk he danced at the Lebret Hotel   what for
no   not really   says he's not writing because they won't
publish his books   he does a number for a book   he
hugged me like I was his old Tibetan guru out on the
dance floor teleporting again

white racists notice color which they don't have   you
might be off-white   a bone white   a cream white
alabaster white   dingy white if you don't wash often
enough   nevermind a non-bleached white   white with
pinkish undertone   peaches and cream   white with
freckles   who is color blind   I write my black ink on
white paper   I white out write out my color lighten up

full of self I saw old whitey again but he wanted to be a
part of a pure religion not like ours   not that he was a
white racist but a pure racist in his heart which had no
color but our color   red   red   mind you a few white
corpuscles but compared to the red they were a minority
not invisible

so few of me yet I still write not for the white audience but
the color of their response to my underclassy class   the
flash of their fit to kill me why race away to the finish
when I cross the finish line will it be white   will I be red
from running   hot and cold touch me not less I am to be
divided against my self who is both red and white but not a
shade of pink maybe a beige pink blushed flushed off
white right I color my winning everytime   I am still in the
red not the black   blackened red   reddened black   but
what about black n' blue   green at the gills   yellow belly
but what about the whitish frightish part I put it behind
behind me when I need to say my piece about togetherness
that we must breed not by ourselves but with everyone
out in the world who will listen   hey   I'm a half a half
breed   a mixed bag breed bread and butter bred my
whole grain bannock will taste as good to me even if I
smear on red jam sink my white teeth down into it down
the red hatch to the black hole   that is behind it all   the
whole black of me   the whore backing up behind me
the sore holy part of me which is the blackest darkest most
colored most non-Indian, non-white slice of me bred to
wonder

TRUCK AND TEAPOT

That blue Chevy truck sitting out back is my friend.
She'll take me to places as long as I keep the spare
tied down with yellow clothes line.

Vulva pressure on chair cushion was released gradually.
Toe grip on the carpet allowed for a slight lift.
My peach tea brews in a reliable brown betty teapot.

I'd offer you a cup if we had the time of day to chat
even longer if you were here in the first place.

Darn kettle's whistle interrupted with winsome sound.
She outdid bagpipes and even tuba straining melodies.

I noticed the leak in her   decided to chuck her out.
She could imitate bagpipe warsongs hesitating on vacuum
whirling and expiring as an old eagle lowers in groan.

I stood ground with bagpipes daring to intrude my poem.
Those steamed up organs were no contest for my writing.

Our songs get pushed up by eagle bone screechy whistling.
If the song ever fades, if dancers slow down their step,
they are made to do double time to get above the ground.

My Indian chants high high higher unwinding road spirals
Old Queen Mary the Scot raises a teapot to her royal lips.

A PAGAN PERFORMS

Indian religion is not for sale. Few manage
to give it away. Each bag of instant medicine
brings its customers. The rush to teach our
traditions leaves me in the dark. Hard to find
time to go back to the blanket or old rugged
cross. Hard to transfer a mother's churchiness.
Her crying lodged in my heart and became company.
She was too hung over. My cup ran over in song.
My little light kept her crooked foot hidden.
A Navajo artist painted his mother's ugly foot.
Each step massages the earth and is walking prayer.
How to account for bunions and callouses like spurs.
Having prayed for my father, my son, ex-husbands,
husbands-to-be I sat myself down to pamper my feet.
Any fool who disturbs a bear fishing is a goner
like the writhing salmon in her jaws. A grizzly
sow humble enough to scoop out a sandbar will nurse
her cubs after fending off the attacking hungry male.

BANANA MOON

Every Indian has a moon he or she
I still have mine tho it's not marked
The time comes, pushing me to change
The calendar so I flip another page

He shaped with his finger a crescent
On his altar of sand and tobacco offerings
He prayed as he worked to define the curves
Of a woman's waist before and after his child

Satisfied when the others would study it
He was still asked to tell them about the moon
As the space was so high, he could razz it up
To me, he said wisely, this is a banana

I wasn't even there to fight for her honor
I had to lie down in my place that night
She spoke in him for us, he just felt her sides
He drew in the moonlight her shadow

I COULD END UP HERE

The West Coast hides old men just the ones to raise hell
in a nursing home with their scars   bleeding heads   just
features to play cards with   I watch Hastings men   they
ask me for a bite and coffee   they earn two quarters
I see them laugh   I say I don't bite   Indian winos work
hard   their shopping cart full of bottled environment
white winos sprawl on sidewalks   seaweed on long beach
shrivelled dicks after the party but I have to ask help
they ignore me   why do I bother them   I'm lost here
looking in back alleys for Vancouver's favorite poet
Chinese kitchen with ducks hanging is near there   I
was told where to get the free meals   I dress too good
the Hong Kong cafe has slow service fifty years ago
the same men run back & forth to the kitchen
now they walk carefully   great grandmother small steps
holding her purse with her loose wrist   I feel lazy
these old buggers work hard   the boiled tongue
on the menu would help me do a smooth reading
I remember the Englishman black eyeliner offering me
tea and oranges   I want Tibetan turquoise in my act
so does Cher   but I'm Indian, I'm an excuse for it

VISITING A POET'S BEDROOM

His Native American literature class was fed their fill;
cauliflowerets, broccoli stems, green onions splayed,
  radish roses, crumbly cheese with green veins.
The wine was delicate not T. Bird or Mad Dog. Not cheap.
His mansion on Summit Drive was shared. Communal living.
  Wealthy Indian lovers we were curious to see more;
  how this people lived; we snuck through the house.
We could use this place for an abused women's shelter.
A butler would service our many visitors; bounce others.
Gentle Indian women laughter went up three floors.

The soiree a success, my white nose grudge got an edge.
I'm drying out. Why blame the wine or vegetables?
He's Hiawatha, Longfellow's boy, come back.
His shabby skin shirt with mangy fringe,
  beads missing; he wore in his youth.
With headband slung, feather drooped, cut-off
  when he passed under a low bridge.
I'm not a Land of the Lakes girl myself.
His bedroom was too neat. I saw he'd gone and covered up
  his typewriter tool with a cute little Navajo rug.

OLD-FASHIONED INDIAN

Sniffing the country in your hair
burning from the woodstove of your lips
brushing a deer running down one leg
feeling porcupine fingers crawling on me

Holding in me the water rings from a bullfrog
jumping your old fur hide blanket for a night
waking you say someone snored in your back

Coming on to me many times a moon today
an old-fashioned Indian trading treaties
sky, water, grub, one more drink or two

Shacking up the old-fashioned way
saving the church collection
peddling your heart on your trail
moving on to another wedding day

WISHBONE DANCING

From the back he looked like a real Indian
Cowboy legs curved wishbone under jeans
Tightly wrapped all the way down each bent bone
Hooked nose craving for a cool breeze
Swaying side to side in a powwow overcrowded
A small butt so he had a pose with his strut
Indian regalia packed and ready to dance 49
Time out for a breather with his side-kick
Fancy Indian dancing — toes pointing always out

CHEEKY MOON

Those eyes show total disgust
at mothers who got sweet talked.
I am the direct result
— fruit of the union —
the big cheek breed
who bucks tradition
becomes a typical troublemaker
except I drink tea
— Blue Ribbon brand —
from a chipped enamel cup.
I should cast dark images
on Grey Owl's guided fantasy.
His beavers led the way
(never mind his wives)
to his imposter identity.

I'm left to defend
one lonely drop of blood.
I might terminate
if I get nosebleed.
The degree never counts
unless you practice law.
I need the law of the land
to respect my blood.
Between you and me
it's the bucket of crabs
pulling us down together.
I count myself lucky
to salvage my ancestry
in this particular drop
at my time.

COLLEGE INDIAN TROUBLE

In college my psych prof diagnosed
my anomie to the class
like all Indians I didn't know the rules:
how to act   either a wild Indian
or a farm girl   I didn't even know
the enema tube was invented by us.
He must have used an inferior brand:
he didn't know we discovered rubber.

CHICKEN IN A MUG

camp out: drag my son to support your protest
   he's afraid it's the usual Indians
     in the park behind shrubbery

Indian lawyer: like to argue myself the point
   getting paid for what you do confused

reaching the public: on t.v. your brand visible
   grabbing your cup & bouillon cube to get
     through a four day fast starving

glamour: California tan the way we used to look
   being outdoors all through the summer
     your trapper coat gripped by nails
       sculptured to rip the skin under

shoot this script: horning in four blocks down
   catch the lady patrol thighs and shoulders
     exposed from her rugged tube dress

sun going down: hurry home to the kitchen cooking
   April days fool you   keemootch times   weather
     not that I mind the coldness of her

MARTYR TONGUE

Mine is a barbecue tongue rolling over
a rotisserie on mesquite coals for flavor.
When I speak at you sister it is a sermon
for we must all kiss the stone of our soup.

We've crouched as we walked bearing babies
on our backs where they fit super snugly.
We have a right to yell in the back lane
"give me back my groceries, my ghetto
blaster" like a guy I heard last night.

Our English is good enough to wipe out
traces of their expression from our mouths.

Four mountain goat years have lapsed for me.
Special sponge grippers in my hooves allow
me to speak without a word slipping foolishly.
An average mountain goat lasts twelve years.

That priest Brebeuf had a speech problem.
He delighted the hell out of his tormentors.
School teachers don't like to admit torture
had a way of creating shame in a young voice.
A tongue had wagged that Brebeuf was a child
molester. How's that for savage gossip.

BLEEDING CHRISTIANITY

Waking up to a West Coast morning, safe
from the blizzard I left behind on the prairie.
Crossing the ocean is simple. Jump in a boat.
It doesn't leap the big waves splashing my face.
Who is blessing me and why do I fear an island?
They have hung their Jesus savior out to dry
on a cross because he tried to swim for it.
Maybe it is just a warning of what they will do.
Priests will catch you. Put thorns on your head.
Your bleeding forehead will remind you of the sin.
Yeah, this sin is that we are to be borne by them.

Indians beheaded a pedophile on Meares Island.
It is a refuge when you think about it.
Did they use a particular name for child molester?
Was he ever called uncle or grandpa at bedtime?
Only a woman companion would I trust in the dark.
He might crawl on the path looking for a face.
The school burned down to the ground leaving
a brass bell and saving an entire generation.
My tendency would be to blame that man unnamed
among us or any woman who lacked God-given balls.
He might have accidently overdone his repenting.

◯

THROWBACK MOON

A singular bump in the Earth gives blessings
over time. Copper gorgets and amulets might
be hammered from the pennies in a piggy bank.
Geechees hid underground beneath their refuse
of sweet potato skins. The world's largest
sweet potato was big as a littered house.
Maroon women peeled plantains even in caves.

In any ruin a mystery remains. Mounds may be
rebuilt. Gourd rattles and pollen dust layer
each woman's occupation. Each midden holds
the answer to how that Early Woman became a
fossil. A throwback chances to emerge from
our untidiness.

WRONG CEREMONY

Even elders have trouble with fame.
Does anyone have a cure for the high?
You think it is time to see an elder.
What do you have to give him,
maybe you'll take yourself or is it too late?
He might look the other way — past you
not into you. Your tobacco is given.
Even if you forget it, he's not forced.
How could anyone refuse your offering?
You want your money's worth and time.
Now you're here, get his autograph.
He's mentioned in a bestseller often.
He might have even written the book.
Knowing that your thigh is tattooed,
a good idea would be to show goose flesh.
Why hide your surface as if we never
get naked with each other to sweat?
But I wonder if you actually have time.
You're busy necking between drags and
asking how far is the nearest airport.
Count all your joints, throw in roaches.
Who flies coach now? Easy reefer answer.
Fame brings them all home to your level,
your altitude, your own ceremony at last.
You might try getting it wrong more often.

WE WERE ALL BUMS ONCE

gopher eating days
sure remember
we all lived in one room
over in Moccasin Flats
Saskatchewan

my love of literature
I found stuck in a box
of *Reader's Digest*
True Confessions
Awake

the best I read
Tortilla Flat
John Steinbeck wrote
I pronounced "els"
as in tor-til-la

I "ee ah" ed after
eating my first tortilla
in L.A. a quarter turned me
Chicana eating taco

back to work
back to how cheap
I was then
now it costs me
a whole powwow
for an Indian taco

HIS KITCHEN

My father was my mother. He took over
cooking and childcare when she left.
At first, our food came from a can.
He wouldn't let me near the kitchen.
I had to learn to cook at school.
He improved. I asked friends over.
He didn't mind. He heaped up potatoes
and gave us canned fruit for dessert.
Only for a short time, did we go out
almost every night to a restaurant.
Even now, I know I am in his kitchen.
A paint scraper sits with the utensils.
I want to put it back with the tools.
It is his egglifter so I know better.
Holiday dinners he cooks and I make gravy.
Hard to forget he's both mother and father.

ONE WAY TO KEEP TRACK OF WHO IS TALKING

If I change one word, I change history. What did I
say today? Do I even remember one word? Writing is
oral tradition. You have to practice the words on
someone before writing it down.

I do not intend to become the world's greatest Indian
orator. Maybe I might by accident. I might speak my
mind even when running off my mouth like I'm doing.
Language finds a tongue. Maybe it will be an Indian
accent.

Counting hostile Indians is made easier because they
don't talk much or very little. They look the part
— the part in the middle with braids. You never do
know if you are talking to an Indian.

Frozen Indians and frozen conversations predominate.
We mourn the ones at Wounded Knee. Our traditions
buried in one grave. Our frozen circles of silence
do no honor to them. We talk to keep our
conversations from getting too dead.

GLOSSARY

Bannock A flat bread, usually baked but sometimes fried.

Booze can A scuzzy after-hours drinking place.

Bungi The incorrect name for Plains Saulteaux or Ojibway, derived from an expression which meant "a little bit"; also referred to "hang-around-the-fort" Indian; anthropological lingo.

Changing Woman A Creatrix for the Navajo people.

Elder A cultural teacher or healer.

49 An after powwow celebration for die-hards.

Geechee Slang for a backwoods Southern black.

Grey Owl An Englishman, known as a protector of beavers, who was effective in being an Indian imposter until his death.

Keemootch On the sly or sneaky.

Maachu Picchu A Peruvian ceremonial centre.

Maroons Slang for Jamaican hill people.

Megwetch Thank you.

Monias Non-Indian.

Moon May mean month of annual cycle or refer to menstrual cycle.

Nichimooses Sweethearts.

Pictographs Rock paintings.

Rez Short for reserve or reservation.

Residential schools Church schools notorious for cultural genocide.

Squaw A derogatory term for a native woman, especially when used by whites. It may also be used in a satirical sense.

Squaw man A slang term for a man who lives with an Indian wife; also used to describe a frontiersman.

Smudge A ritual to purify participants for ceremonies.

Sweetgrass A braided, fragrant grass used as incense.

Throat singer An Inuit woman singer.

Wike Muskrat root.

Waboose Rabbit.

Certain Saulteaux/Cree words are written in their Anglicized form.